Pieces of Soul

Francine Nguyen-Savaria

BookLeaf Publishing

Presentation by *BookLeaf Publishing*

Web: www.bookleafpub.com

E-mail: info@bookleafpub.com

ISBN: 978-93-95784-97-9

First edition 2022

To my husband.

ACKNOWLEDGEMENT

To my husband Matthieu who sees charm and poetry in everything I do, even on my least poetic days: Thank you for believing in me and my abilities to fulfill any dream and vision placed before me. I am forever grateful for your incredible support in all of my endeavours and your understanding of my unconventional artistic path. Our married life remains our greatest and most precious artwork.

To Arlene: Thank you for encouraging me to share my expressivity with the world through artistic writing. I am grateful for our friendship, our shared love for literature and our inspiring exchanges.

To Frank who watched me grow into the artist I am, who received many, many pieces of my soul with gentleness and care, who supported me along the way and whose shared piece of soul I still carry with me today: I would not have dared writing poetry in my second language, had you not seen the soul of a poet in me. You are a lighthouse in my life. Thank you, for everything.

PREFACE

These twenty-one poems were written as a part of the publisher's "The Write Angle" challenge: one poem a day for twenty-one days. They were jotted down on a corner of the kitchen counter, on bus rides, during walks, sitting on the front steps of churches and cathedrals, anywhere, when words would come to me. They delve into the depth of friendship, fears, betrayal, loss, grief, compassion, search of self and the mysteries of beauty and love.

Poetry is emotion set to the rhythm of words and the mind's symbols. Writing daily, under the pressure of time, was an intense inner path. It pointed to deep truths and confirmed my life-long fascination for water, ships and bridges as well as my love for winter. Several Montreal landmarks and elements of my daily life also appeared along the way.

These poems are pieces of my soul I sometimes wish I could have shared personally with loved ones, but did not get a chance to. Some things are difficult to convey in a normal conversation or an email, and poetry is alas not always called for... A friend once encouraged me to write, telling me that even though my words might not convey anything to the person they were destined to, they could still touch someone else's heart. I therefore hope that somehow, my personal journey meets yours.

Absence

I miss you.

I utter the words
And the space in the air
Thins to the faded silhouette of absence
Of silence, too.

Laughter echoes in distant shades of blue
And the quiet gift of a piece of soul
The blackness of words typed from lands afar
Find a voice
A loyal companion I carry in my soul.

The words surfaced
In bonds wrongly bonded
On waves of loneliness
On tides of loss and arid shores
On lakes of dreams and on visions of hope.

The piece of soul you shared
A golden heart, crowned with white petals of
quiet reverence,
I have grown to its guiding light
A Northern Star
But, oh, so far away, when I was yet a child!

That piece of soul survived
Raging fires of fierce fears
Voices of shame, and bleeding thorns of fainted hopes
The never-ending questions of the soul:
Am I too much?
Am I clinging to the firmament of a dim and cherished light
Something long gone?

Am I like the moon,
Shining the light of a reflected sun afar
On pieces of myself?
But the moon, at night, is beautiful in the velvet skies
Perhaps I, too, shine in reflection of other stars
From all broken pieces left with me.

I miss you.

As I utter the words,
You speak to me in ten thousand whispers
In the chant of fountains
In scattered silences
Of painted golden stars
In holy communion of common gestures
To the beauty of the unsaid
Unnamed
Un-shown

In eternal quest
Of glimpses of heaven.

You speak to me with the voice from before
In February's biting wind
In solitude's shadow
And the space so close to heart
The well of ink I dip in
And rain unto paper like shattered pieces of soul.

You speak to me in sparkles of wonder
Have I so changed?
It seems to me that I can touch the memory
Or is it the treasured weight of love
I carry in my heart?

That piece of soul that you have left with me,

It bloomed.

The Outcast

This morning, I saw a homeless man
Pigeons feeding from his extended hand
On crumbs of filthy crusts of bread
Ten or twelve, I think they were
In all shades of busting city dirt
Feasting forgetfully, fighting for their turn.

The man was still, and so was I
On the corner, watching in wonder
As he made friends in tender offer
Of what was dropped by passers-by.

As I watched him simply being
He transformed, but for a moment
There was a child, perhaps, who rose
In the midst of shattered bottles
Raw, untamed, unquenchable beauty
Rising like the sun onto the city's roofs.

Soon, the crumbs returned to restless footsteps
And the begging resumed
But there, ever shining in rags of misery
Stood an untouched piece of soul.

Stay

The ship had departed.

And now, the heart laid bare on the kitchen
counter
Sleepless nights had clung to dawn's delusion
As time brutally swept the joy of reunion
Now impossible
Drowning its sorrow in cups of bitter cocoa
Sobbing in weariness of a worn out story
As, indifferent, winter slowly thawed.

It had spent days, weeks, in heavy quietness
Traces of past trauma
Of banter taking too deep a root
In teasing's part of truth
In fear of being shelved as it dared uncover
The source of its light
In trembling expectation of being turned away
And running home, to barbed wire fences
Unknown
Unmet
But its own voice whispered: "Stay."

Days had passed, in endless questions
In harsh observation
Of one's inmost desires
Gratitude for offerings past

And fears. Why did you matter so?

It shivered in the cold gray morning, that fragile piece of soul
Unveiled to beat and pulse
An offering wild and free
Of tenderness, silence, and profound affection
And perhaps of self, too, in intense fireworks
Of unbounded colours and delightful laughter
Suddenly wrapped in cloaks of deep blue velvet hue.

Under droplets of coolness and busy exhaustion
And too tight a life's space
The piece of soul pleaded:
"If you will carry me, I promise, I will be very small.
I will speak the language of world's mundanities
And ask so little of your time, you will barely notice
For all I wish, is to walk by your side. Will you let me?"

But then it laughed. It was a sad laughter:
"Small? Small I can't be.
I will ever explode in useless beauty."
Tears flowed down the river of the missed encounter
Flashes of unworthiness piled on scars of rejection
And unreceived gift of self.

It shivered in distance of hasty sentences
Faint echoes of dismissiveness
And spaces between words
Of what was not said, much more than what was
said
It shivered now, with clenched teeth:
"What are they all afraid of?
Poetry is ever only the music of the words
The expression of dance transfixed upon the
page
The way they fold around contours of secrecy
The subtle warming to blazing truth...
Leave, leave, let the ship sink while they won't
look,
Passion is your language, and contemplation too.
Leave, forget, and shine
You can't be, otherwise."

But leave, it could not.

Now, it wished it had the strength of wrath
The breastplate of anger
The haughtiness of pride
For protection
Slamming doors onto cold, icy walls
Of guilt: "I always make the wrong choices."

- What are you holding onto?, asked the risen
sun.

- The beauty of a fleeting gaze, met at the great portal,
The unhindered joy, in surprise's appearance
Standing in the doorframe, still wet from evening's rain.
"Stay. Stay, but for a moment. A little longer.
Stay for friendship's sake," whispered the soul.
And of course, now, it forgot what it were to say
At the possible sight of your extended ear.
Or perhaps not.
The heart laid bare on the kitchen counter,
With words essential:
"I love you very much."

A red Cardinal sang, in melodious whistles
As it were, every morning,
A reminder of a well deep within
Where steadfastness of love
Is the heart's own treasure
Untouchable.
And the soul waited, vulnerable, yet wild
It stayed, for hope, perhaps,
And because it mattered,
And because it was true.

The Boatman and the Bridge-Builder

Once upon a time, far in Orient, lived a boatman.
His eyes had seen the sun rising over the mountains
Forever
For centuries, he had taken people on his boat
Across the foggy lake.
What was on the other side?
No one knew
A little house, perhaps,
Fruit trees, and a sand garden
And fog,
Fog, day and night.

One thing, one thing only, did one know:
Those who crossed the lake would never come back
And yet, each day, people paid the boatman,
Crossing to unknown shores
Forever.
When they could not pay, they left some token,
Promising they would come back
But none ever came back

None waited for the boatman
On the other side.

The boatman kept in his house
A box of jewelry
Miscellaneous items
Of faded memories
He never sold them
For he secretly hoped that someone would come back
To pay
Or really, to tell him what was beyond
Beyond the house, the garden, and the fruit trees
For he himself did not know
He was too afraid
That he, too, would never come back.

Each night, when his work was done,
And the sun was down,
And the moon rose,
The boatman tied his rowboat to a tree
And sang
As he watched birds fly over the garden
And the little house
On the other side.

The birds were colourful but they never sang
Each night, he wondered if he were not the boatman of death,

The Reaper leading all to lands of rest
From which they never returned
As his boat was a one-way boat.

And each night, as he watched the birds and sang,
He recalled those he had taken aboard
He sang of the blue sky and the blooming roses,
Of joy and sorrow, love and loss...
And none listened.

One night, when he had sung, and the birds had vanished
He saw a dim light on the other side
He sat there, watching, as the light grew closer.

Suddenly, over the lake appeared a splendid bridge,
All made out of paper.
On the bridge stood a child holding a lantern
The little boy walked over and stood before him.

The bridge vanished into thin air.

- I know you. You are the boatman.
- Who are you?
- I am the bridge-builder.
- Do you live in the house, across the lake?

But the little boy did not answer.
He gazed over the lake.

- I build bridges so people can cross.
- I never saw a soul coming back.
- No one ever comes back. It is a one-way bridge.
- I never saw people walking on bridges...
I never saw a bridge over the lake before.
- They cross when you are asleep.
- How will you return?
- You will take me on your boat. What is your price?
- Nothing. People who don't pay won't come back anyway.
- I am happy I saw this shore. It is beautiful.
- What is on yours?

The little boy did not answer
He only smiled.

The boatman brought him across the lake
The boy walked across the garden
Leaving no footprint on the sand
Then, he vanished into the fog.

The following night, the boatman did not return
He waited in silence for the bridge-builder to appear

The night was cold
There were no birds.

Soon enough, the little boy came
Holding his lantern and some blue paper
With silver stars on it
He folded it into a bridge and threw it in the waters
The bridge appeared.

People walked to the bridge, one by one
Before they could cross, they murmured into his ear
The bridge-builder smiled and led them across, holding his lantern.

Trembling, the boatman left his boat and walked towards the house
Leaving footprints on the sand
He turned around
His boat had vanished
The boatman walked past the fruit trees
On the other side
The sand garden never seemed to end
It was calm, peaceful, and so mysterious
And then, he noticed paper birds on the ground
He walked to the house
It was made of paper
The door was open

But the house was empty
The boatman walked away.

The little boy was waiting for him.

- What is your price?, said the boatman.
- Tell me a story. Your story.
- You know my story, I am the boatman.
- Then, sing. When you sing, my birds can fly.

So, the boatman sang
And the paper birds flew.
The little bridge-builder threw a bridge over the lake
And silently led the boatman home,
Where his rowboat had returned,
Waiting for him.

The following day, the boatman's song told stories of paper bridges,
Birds and little boys.

When the moon rose, the boatman sang again
The birds flew
The lantern and bridge appeared.
The boatman did not wait
He ran over the bridge while it was still there
He expected to meet hundreds of people crossing

The other way.
Instead, he met only a lady holding a lantern
Her eyes were the same as the little boy's.

- Who are you?
- I am the bridge-builder. You walked in my garden and left footprints on the sand.
- Isn't the bridge-builder a little boy?
Though the boatman knew the answer,
The lady did reply:
- I appear as a little boy to those who cross the bridge...
The other way.
- What is your price?
- There is no price tonight.

The lady smiled and turned her back
The boatman stood on the bridge and watched.
The birds became real.
When he turned around to find his boat,
It had vanished
And the bridge was made of stone.

The Chessboard

Giant chessboards stand on Sainte-Catherine
Street
Moments of magic amidst commercial haste
Summer's joy lingering on life-sized pieces
People, observant, comment and point
They shout and hint
They are Bonaparte, watching
Moving their toy armies
To strategized victory.

I once fancied chess, did you know?
A game of intellectual prowess
Of fast thinking
An ethical combat in near chivalrous rules
A mind-master's game
Controlling fire, taking turns
Taking King Arthur's conquering knights
To the tile floor of Westminster Abbey.

But then, dragged into the chess of life
Where rules slightly differed
And allies could change sides
Where hearts bled and conquering blinded
A pawn rising to queen
I felt the weight of centuries

Shaking the rooks
Of necessary power.

Now, too weary for chessboard games,
I stand by and watch the Bonapartes-to-be
I sit and befriend Poetry by my side
As they get lost into deep thinking's tide.

The Spider

She extended her hand
Fighting back the urge of disgust
"Climb," she said softly
"Are you afraid of me?" the spider asked
"A little," said the girl. "You are enormous...
And not very pretty."
"But I have velvety feet, and symmetrical
shapes!" gasped the creature
It was offended, now.
"Indeed. But isn't beauty in the eye of the
beholder?
- Why don't you kill me already? Why extend
your hand?
- There is no jar in sight. And out, I must bring
you
Before you meet Father's deadly slipper!"

They sat for a while on the porch.
Before it returned to its artful canevas
Of silk and dew,
The spider raised once more its watchful globes.

"Why have you spared me? You don't even like
me.

- Why kill? I will not eat you, nor will you clothe me,
Your bites can't poison, and your kin won't invade.
I have no use for killing
And steep is the price of murder.
Sure, you are not aesthetically pleasing
— To the human eye — she added carefully.
Really, you are but only a mere inconvenience
And the door is so close by.
- But it is more effort, isn't it?
Humans squish my people.
More efficient, they say.

- Bollocks. Shall I take a life, out of sheer laziness?
I could never see myself in a mirror again!
I know what it is, to be out of our place
Walked on and trampled down
An inconvenience.
If those who find me so could crush me with their heel
I would be dead several times already!"

The spider considered this strange voice of mercy
Speaking not quite fondly, not quite full of pity.
Perhaps, it thought, in spite they be ugly
The human heart is not all hard and hideous.

Ships Passing in the Night

Ships passing in the night
A blind date, but not a date:
A stranger offering a seat
In the crowded café
Where I stood alone with my plate
And nowhere to lay it down
"Will you sit a while with me?
- Thank you. - Let's talk; do you read?"

Blue-eyed chocolate lover,
Little did he know
He offered me our missed encounter
And perhaps another failed one, too
From another place, another time, another town
As snow fell on snow
Winter's victorious return
On late April's morning.

Conversation flows
From his mouth, that is
I think of everything, but too late
Thoughts do not bloom upon my speech
As they seek the soil of silence
They stumble in timid words

Fading with winter left outside
And lighten at the touch of nostalgia.

What is nostalgia?
The memory of a voice that speaks
Long after silence fell
The voice I hear in printed words
The voice of white silence
My fondness for amaretto:
The flavour of gelato that remained
From the last coffee we had together.

I remember the question you asked:
"What is your greatest dream?"
And I dare ask the blue-eyed stranger
He laughs, and says he loves people
Talking to people
Meeting people
Helping people
Coffee with people.

The social beast meets the poet
A siren breaks morning's silence
The ships have sailed
They departed the port
A lonely sight on the misty river
What is nostalgia?
Tenderness and memory's child
Or joy's flowers on grief's tomb?

The ships passed in the night
They glided on emerald waters
One, large, stable and faithful
The other, leaping on restless tides
I rehearse our missed encounter
Memories of questions unanswered:
What do you live for?
What keeps you awake at night?

In another universe
I ran into you
And gave you joy's embrace
In another universe, the ships have met
There wasn't ice on the river
And winter's wind was mild
But never, in any universe
Life has made you otherwise.

Ocean claimed both ships as the rising sun
Parted moving waters
Both set to unknown shores
Ships passing in the night
"I will be back," said the small one.

Silence

Silence
Space in the veil of time
The world hushes after a snowfall
Vast, white quietness all around

Silence
The sound of Christmas morning
Simmering on firewood
In grandma's pots of applesauce

Silence
Voices from the soul
In the empty church
Uninterrupted beauty of reverence

Shall I confess that I kneel
Before the Blessed Sacrament
Perhaps not so much to adore
But for silence's comforting blanket?

Silence
When evening turns blue
Rests in the eyes of my lover
In tender words unspoken

Silence
Eloquence of gestures
In slumber of the words
Heaven's gift to the soul.

I Was Born to Winter

I was born to winter
Vast, intense and wild
Arid plains of loneliness
Winter harsh and cold
But also soft and quiet
Bitter and fierce
But also all heart's warmth
And comforting wool blankets.

Paths of mischievous ice
Slippery sidewalks
Dragged into city's dirty streets,
Frozen engines
Cars that would not start
And no place to park,
I am winter.

But I am, too, the stillness of morning
The ray of sunshine broken into
A thousand sparkling tones
The lightness of snow
And the birds' singing free
I am long dark nights
But also Northern lights
Advent's hope

Christmas' joy
And waves of nostalgia.
Freezing, deathly winds
And salty boots
But also the crackling of the fireplace
And the silence of snow.

I was born to winter
I am bold, biting winds
And delicate snowflakes,
I reign on Solstice
Independent and mighty,
Snowing fragile pieces of soul.

The Bridge of Fear

I walk on Champlain Bridge
A pilgrimage on my inner bridges
Bridges unfinished
Bridges old and bridges new
A piece of the old bridge
Stands alone in the middle
Awaiting to be removed
To be taken down.

Am I that structure of steel
Loyal and faithful to the end
But holding nothing,
Standing alone?

Afar, a boat passes, unbothered.

Should I dismantle the old bridge?
Should I let the ships drift apart?
They would still be whole, but oh, such a sad story!
Is our time past and gone
A memory meant to be treasured
Like a pressed flower in a book
Rather than a rosebush to tend and bloom?
Is my bridge destined to fall?

I look into the grey waters
They seem so still and yet they hold
Deep, complex tides
Did you know there are skilled pilots
For each section of the deadly river?
It really is a job!
They take the Captain's seat
Aboard the ships.

One says that love can never be understood, only fear
I look down far below
I dive into my greatest fear
I know it, like none else
I have felt it, danced with it,
Flirted with it even
I am the pilot aboard the ship:
I think you ought to know
My greatest fear
Is to leave this world
Not having loved enough
Or not well enough
— What an irony!

I often wish you knew
How much I fear bothering you
How many times I draft my words
In my mind
Before they dare flee to you

I fear taking your time
I fear you see what I am not:
Another Emma Bovary
A stage artist lacking her crowd.
But then, unhappy, I walk the bridge again
For what is friendship,
If I can't offer you what is most beautiful to me?
A piece of life
Art, song
Peace in chanting and words affirming
A piece of my life
Or heart?

I walk on bridges of fear
Rising above troubled waters:
Taking too much space
Asking for too much
Being in the way
My emails filling your inbox
Like pebbles a pocket
Voicemail piling
Upon vacation's return.

I wish silence wasn't so invisible
And the bridge could speak on its own
I wish I could know
Without the aid of words
You see, I do not trust myself
What if, I think, I really did it all

Only to impress?
What if I really wanted to conquer
And not give?
What if I am lying
Unbeknown to myself?
I imagine impatience
Annoyance
"Oh, again."
And I retreat.

Strong winds blow my hair
Into disorganized knots
I walk the bridge tentatively
As if it could not hold my weight
Mind you, the old bridge
Was about to fall.

Perhaps, by now, you are laughing
At low self-worth's words of folly
I walk the bridge, past
Islands of rest and city structure
Cars pass by, at full speed
So do my thoughts,
Over and over.

Am I driving you away?
Can I once disclose my soul
Without doing so?
Misunderstanding laughs at me

I walk to the high structure point
The bridge’s white crown
An iceberg in the sky
An act of faith
What is my heart after?

Deep down, it says, I wish I knew
That the bridge mattered to you
That I truly bring you joy
That I touch your life
For the better...
Still.
Really, it's all I wish I knew
And I would go my merry way
On Champlain Bridge,
Simply being.

Sunrise

- How do you know if the sun is rising? Sunrise and sunset are so alike!

- I know that the sun is rising, for I am sailing towards East.

The Inner Child

They come in
Voices from the past
Hushed and forgotten
Ghosts in the mirror
Voices murmuring
Memories of happy days
Wills of ambition, of the harsh desire
To prove herself.

"Look," they whisper "at so and so
Models so admired
None can equal such gifts,
Such grace."
Is it pride or fear of shame?
Or fear of seing her failure
Draped in realistic tones?
"These are the ones destined to succeed."
They point at the brilliance of those so far ahead.

"Not good enough," scorns
The ghost of errors glistening
Worms of shame
In failure to succeed
"What happened?" they say
Pride comes in spurs of fear

Shining mirages of fame and gold
Lure the eyes she is seeking to meet
And they get thrown at her:
Pebbles of stable jobs
Nine-to-fives, ideas of seriousness
Of a life worth living
"How much does it pay?"
"Have you got enough work?"

"Indeed. I am exhausted
Emotionally exhausted,"
But that, she can't say.

Fight-or-flight seizes her
Breathless attacks
Everything is quick sands
"What if I fail? What if I cover myself in shame
Never to live again from offerings of beauty
What if I stumble?"
She falls
She collapses
Those voices from the past
They don't speak
They grab her by the throat
On days meant for feast and joy
They talk through her trembling hands
Blurred vision
Racing heart and cold sweats

Loss of path
And perhaps loss of self.

But every time, she rises
With unquenchable thirst
Of breaking free
Arise, O Child within!
Pull out thy sword against the voices
Of well-meaning
Showing you endlessly
What you ought not to be!

The flame burns still,
Her rebellion is a cloak
On the deep blue ancient soul
Who tenderly marvels
At roses and fountains
Who loves in abundant
Fields of wildflowers
Endless pieces of heart
Castles, universes, fireworks of affection
Entirely
Without question.

She wants to drink, carefree
From golden chalices
To splash unto the world
Drops of sacredness
Untamed, fierce and free

To live from flowing wine
Of eternal beauty.

She wants to let it flow like boiling blood
Unto paper
Into song, into dance
She is a whirlwind of passion
"No, I will not be your fears!"
She shouts to the world
She rises to stand again
And again
Battling the ghosts in the mirror
Undefeated
Braver than gifted, really
Facing fears like burning demons,
Fighting to break free
And be.

My Secret Garden

My secret hiding place
Is a garden that tops a hill,
A hill itself
Sinuous paths of bushes
And statues of sorrow
Sights of redemption.

I like it best in the morning
When none is in sight
Save for the gardener
Has he been, once, robed in white
And bearing wings?

There is no empty tomb,
But a fountain in the middle
Fenced off,
Flowers all around
And a golden lamb, too.

Down below lies the city
A promised land in slumber
Lo! It awakens
And pilgrims climb
To the mountain's sanctuary
Stillness is troubled.

I leave my secret hiding place
Shielding its blooming treasures
I walk down to the city,
Bringing its peace with me.

The Reaper

When I first met the Reaper
I was not twenty-one
She had come for a man
Right at the church's door.

She wasn't stealthy or even serene
She came with loud sirens
The life was fetched from our arms
Before my very eyes
The ambulance's door shut tight
The Reaper had come first.

The man was nameless to me
A joyful wave was all it was
Before I sat at the keyboards
Once, a photo was taken
"Cheese!" We smiled. Click.

The funeral came and the urn brought in
I knew nothing of him
And played the chosen hymns,
As duty called before.

"Look!" called a voice
My heart missed a beat

There, on the table, stood
A lonely photo:
The familiar smiles captured
On a Sunday
Which Sunday?
The memory of a rare friend
On this shore of the sea
Had I known, he would have had a name
And sweeter memories, too.

Still, today, I wonder
Of souls who pass before my eyes
For what is an encounter,
If not a piece of Time
Stolen from the Reaper?

Unanswered Question

Of all possible means
Why did you choose the gun?
Symbol?
Availability, knowledge, proficiency?
Or quick and efficient
A cry for help so short
None could respond
In time?
An assurance
A departure
A flight?
Or was it — I think it is —
The cry, desperate
Of those who have lost hope and faith
That one can hear, even?

I hear the cringe, already
The shiver of disbelief:
"Why such a gory question?"
So many questions left
Unanswered
And I would ask that one?
Guilt of survivors
Resentment, anger
Grief

Loss
I remain silent:
Useless to question
The living.

Judgment meets blame
Encounters compassion
In voices trying to soothe
The one, everlasting question:
Why?
What pushed you over edge?
And yet, it seems to me
That if I knew why the gun
I could piece everything,
Understand.

For I know all too well
The weariness of the soul
Exhaustion of the heart
Implosion of all
We can no longer bear
"I get it" they say
We never were so close
But had I known, for being closer
I could have seen the path untrod
For desire to live howls
Until it breaks.

How are you?
Fine, thank you
I am exhausted
Exhausted of drama
Other lives' drama
Shaping the road
Feeding on calm
Pushing away
Tired of explaining ascension to beauty
The sleeplessness of rest
Wounds that seem nothing
The weight invisible
Others can't see
Or understand
"They are better off without me."

See?

Your soul might not have spoken
Words similar
The idea is the same
Breaking point.

Covid isolation
Masks and hopelessness
All too close
All too hard
All too heavy
Life so far, unreachable

Warmth untouchable
Problems piled upon themselves
Remoteness of watchful eyes
That could have seen.

Were you trying to hold it at gun point?
Depression
Before it became terminal?
Had there been thoughts of love
Of care?
Answers awaiting, afar
Why the nauseating question
When so many are left?
And yet, I have only one
For means tell more than reason
And if the gun could speak
I could perhaps turn back
And prevent it from shouting.

— *With love. Requiescat in pace.*

The Butterfly and the Rose

There was something familiar in the Butterfly's smile.
The Rose recognized the Caterpillar.
"I did not know this side of you," she said.
"It takes time to unveil me," replied the Butterfly.

Inner Hug

Eyes closed
A slight weight
A memory held close
Warmth in my arms and on my cheek
The space in the air fills
A hand closes on my heart
It becomes real
For a moment
I hug the thought of you.

The Black Sheep

The black sheep looks up from the shelf
Little ears perking
Eyes charming
The plushy creature, in the palm of her hand
Longs for love transforming.

A life, a voice, a mischief
Lo! It stretches its embroidered smile
"We are meant to belong!
If you will feed me gelato
And perhaps hot cocoa
I will be your black sheep
The voice of your soul."

"Let me sleep 'till noon
I am dreamier than most
But an artist too
I listen to none
And I baa out of tune
Also, I am soft on the cheek
Will you adopt me?"

She tries to resist, but the voice
Bouncy and spicy makes her smile
And she knows he is her white one's twin.

All the fluffy sheep
The Little Prince refused!
Warm and a bit odd
The little sheep unwanted
Left to live on paper
And in a child's mind.

Little sheep so real
Comforting and warm
With watchful, tender eyes,
Each with its own voice
Dreaming of gardens
Called by fountains
Coping with rejection
In quirks and sparkly manners
Laughter and inappropriateness
Deliciously, childishly mischievous
They say what they will.

An army of soft paws
Drying tears, comforting hearts
Fluffy voices to answer
The deep cut of words
Or absence of words
Funny smiles and expressive faces
Always out of place
Out of time
Out of rankings:
The arms of a poet

Companions to the soul
Loyal to heart's Child
They raise their silly voices
Demanding bliss of carelessness
Tones of confidence
Soulful truths.

"You are a black sheep."
She is a black sheep, isn't she?
"If you will feed me gelato...
I will show you carefreeness
And quirkiness.
Be yourself. Be like me."
Ah, little fluffy sheep
Telling the soul to be
All that it is
All that it needs
Stitched with love and care.

"It's half price."
Her husband smiles as she hesitates
He takes the creature and pays
"Baa, baa" the sheep rejoices
But only she can hear
And the black sheep joins the flock of the free
The stuffed toys so Real
To the Poet's mind.

The Gift

I once gave a precious gift:
To see me falling in love,
A key to a secret garden
And such a fragile piece of heart
A free fall of the level-headed.

Not that it was much to the eye
To watch the meeting of souls
From across oceans, afar,
But a gift of trust, it was
A secret so guarded
A kiss, caught in the deserted hallway,
Had been the front page event
Of gossipers.

Love birds hiding,
The timid heart sharing
The innocent confidence
Shielded by distance
Until sunflowers grew
A secret of ordinary things
A sight so often seen
It could have been cliché
But it was much more, too:
Commitment and search, already,

For bonds of depth
Without words, yet, to explain.

The recipient, in time,
Returned the gift carefully kept
In words of gladness and joy
Of a witness to the bond
Fastened well and tight
In roses blossoming
Over the garden walls.

Letting Go

I open my hand
The wind blows away
Soft feathers of music
Yet, the timber of fondness
Remains in heart's chest.

A blue balloon blown towards dreams,
Bubbles rise and fly
Home, to starlit heavens
I let go and yet retain
Love, in heart's well
Letting go to lands of joy
Yet building a home within
Heart's home, anywhere,
Letting fly, and letting be
A new sun in the skies.

Letting go and keeping, still
Holding hands on shores afar
Walking paths, side by side
Common footsteps and roads crossing
Love growing, steadfast
Tending to branches reaching
And the roots linking
Heart to heart

Letting pain go, so love will stay
To become its destiny.

I open my hand
A wandering star flees,
Finding the Milky Way
Treasuring love's bond
In common skies touching.

September Afternoon

Summer slowly fades away
Have you noticed how everything is brighter
In September's low afternoon rays?
Golds and red earth are warmer
The sky seems nearer
The leaves blush ever so slightly
The crimson chrysanthemum wears its royal mantle
The late summer days speak
Of the last time you said "I hope to see you
Soon,"
Nearly a year ago
As Autumn set in.

I will come to you.

Tomorrow, when the sun will set
I will walk towards you
Although you do not know
But you might have guessed
I will walk and carry Autumn's light:
Maybe, to my heart, it will be a burial
Crowned with new life's joy
The setting of a sun

Behind distance's veil
At least in this world.

My heart beats
In joy's expectation
And rejection's apprehension
All at once
Does it matter, still?
The sun breaks the clouds like a broken promise
Mourned by crickets
How much is loyalty worth?
I asked the fountain
It is worth the promise of Spring
The majesty of Autumn
An Equinox of truth
And beauty.

I will come to you.

Sometimes, the light is most beautiful
When it fades
Is it the end?
I fear what I will meet
Forgive me:
I am wounded
There have been first and last encounters
In Autumn's light
Friends drinking to ending
And it tasted of shame

But dim light is soft, too...
I will honour such a light
I will be the chrysanthemum
And the cold breeze
And the warm rays I will shed
On my world unknown.

If you asked the fountain in the rose garden
It would tell you of tears shed on a lost friend
And how those tears somehow
Bore a piece of you too
It would tell a tale
Too long for its contents
It would tell you of slowness
And necessary time
To listen to my soul
And perhaps, just to live
It would tell you of wounds
Its clear waters soothed
And the traces fresh
In souls that could not meet
Without deep tearing.

It was meant to be:
Autumn turning to winter
But the line is blurry
Between what ought and what wants to be
A sea so deep, and so hard to explain
In the end, what was the night made of?

What comes before us,
Where we stand in one's eyes
On that unwritten list of constellations
Of commitments
Godly truth and depth of heart
The force that displaces joy
Of the souls' encounter
The Compass' true North:
Do our Norths align?

The fountain talks endlessly in whispers
It would tell you, too,
Of me, giving thanks for you
Of how you offer me
Your visions of heaven
And how I offer you the whispers of my soul
Please, please, tread softly
You walk on broken ground
But wounds also shed light,
Softer.

The fountain is far, now
But on a hill close-by
Other waters chanting
Cannot hold their secrets
If you listen closely
They will narrate my tale:
September's light could not be
Had you not come to me

Beauty matters
It is one language of Heaven.

Tomorrow, when the sun will set
I will come to you with September's light
And honour the deep beauty
Of all you are to me.

www.ingramcontent.com/pod-product-compliance
Lightning Source LLC
Chambersburg PA
CBHW051735130826
49812CB00033B/871
9789395784979